19

Golf Duffer's Diary for the 19th Hole

Mary Susan Carey

Golf Duffer's Diary from the 19th Hole

Mary Susan Carey

Copyright © 2019. All Rights Reserved.

No part of this book may be reproduced or transmitted in any form or by any means, including but not limited to information storage and retrieval systems, electronic, mechanical , photography, recording, etc., without the written, dated, and signed, permission of the copyright holder, Angel Journal and Mary Susan Carey.

Although the author and publisher have prepared this document with the greatest of care, and have made every effort to preserve the accuracy of its contents, we assume no responsibility or liability for errors, inaccuracies or omissions.

Published by Angel Journal and Books,

Burlington, ON, Canada

First Edition: First Printing

ISBN: 978-1-9994486-6-0

If found, please contact:

Name:
_____

Tel:
_____

Email:
_____

MY TARGETS

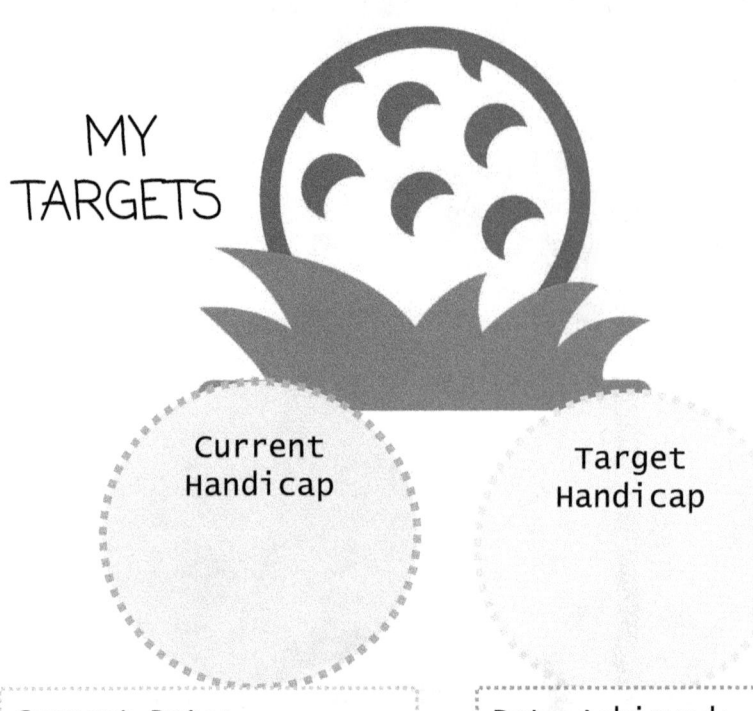

Current Handicap

Target Handicap

Current Date:

Date Achieved:

Current Averages	
Fairways Hit	
GIRs	
Up & Downs	
3-Putts	
No./Putts	
Penalties	
Average Score	

Target Averages	
Fairways Hit	
GIRs	
Up & Downs	
3-Putts	
No./Putts	
Penalties	
Target Score	

MY YARDAGES

Date:

CLUB	HEAD WIND	TAIL WIND	NO WIND
Driver			
3-Wood			
3-Hybrid			
4-Hybrid			
5-Iron			
6-Iron			
7-Iron			
8-Iron			
9-Iron			
Pitching Wedge			
Gap Wedge			
Sand Wedge			
Lofted Wedge			

Areas for improvement

Notes on progress

MY TARGETS

Current Handicap

Target Handicap

Current Date:

Date Achieved:

Current Averages	
Fairways Hit	
GIRs	
Up & Downs	
3-Putts	
No./Putts	
Penalties	
Average Score	

Target Averages	
Fairways Hit	
GIRs	
Up & Downs	
3-Putts	
No./Putts	
Penalties	
Target Score	

Date:

CLUB	HEAD WIND	TAIL WIND	NO WIND
Driver			
3-Wood			
3-Hybrid			
4-Hybrid			
5-Iron			
6-Iron			
7-Iron			
8-Iron			
9-Iron			
Pitching Wedge			
Gap Wedge			
Sand Wedge			
Lofted Wedge			

Areas for improvement

Notes on progress

MY TARGETS

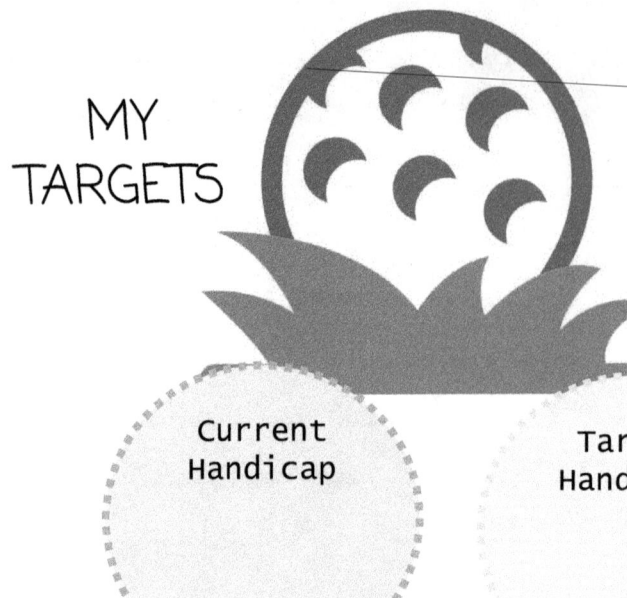

Current Handicap

Target Handicap

Current Date:

Date Achieved:

Current Averages	
Fairways Hit	
GIRs	
Up & Downs	
3-Putts	
No./Putts	
Penalties	
Average Score	

Target Averages	
Fairways Hit	
GIRs	
Up & Downs	
3-Putts	
No./Putts	
Penalties	
Target Score	

MY YARDAGES

Date:

CLUB	HEAD WIND	TAIL WIND	NO WIND
Driver			
3-Wood			
3-Hybrid			
4-Hybrid			
5-Iron			
6-Iron			
7-Iron			
8-Iron			
9-Iron			
Pitching Wedge			
Gap Wedge			
Sand Wedge			
Lofted Wedge			

Areas for improvement

Notes on progress

MY TARGETS

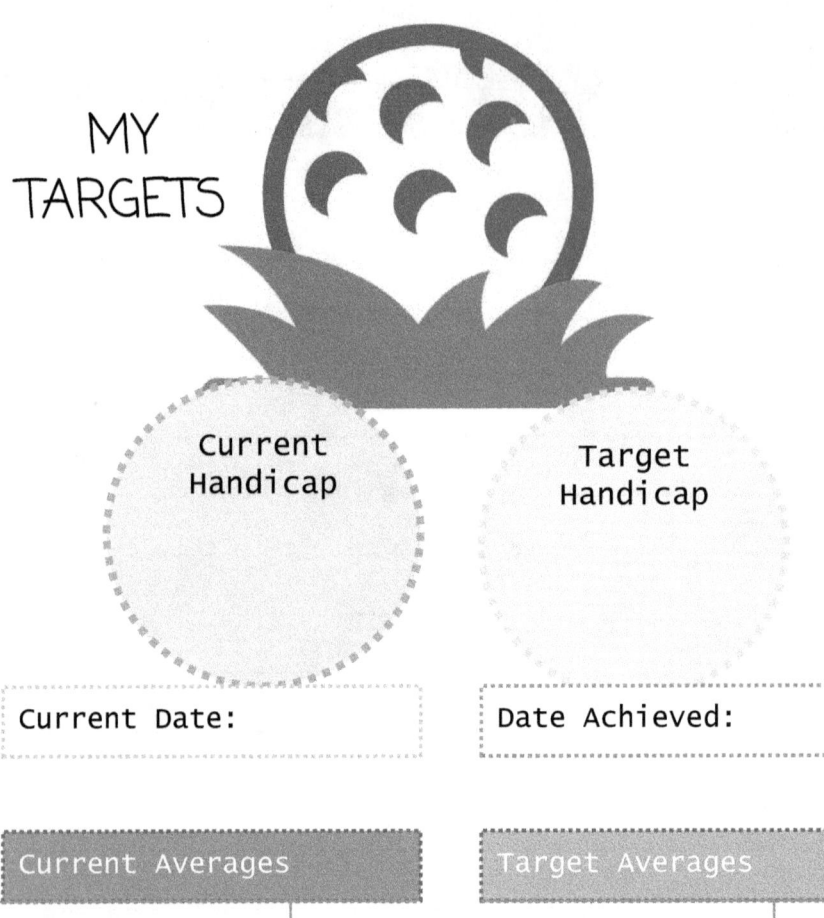

Current Handicap

Target Handicap

Current Date:

Date Achieved:

Current Averages	
Fairways Hit	
GIRs	
Up & Downs	
3-Putts	
No./Putts	
Penalties	
Average Score	

Target Averages	
Fairways Hit	
GIRs	
Up & Downs	
3-Putts	
No./Putts	
Penalties	
Target Score	

Date:

CLUB	HEAD WIND	TAIL WIND	NO WIND
Driver			
3-Wood			
3-Hybrid			
4-Hybrid			
5-Iron			
6-Iron			
7-Iron			
8-Iron			
9-Iron			
Pitching Wedge			
Gap Wedge			
Sand Wedge			
Lofted Wedge			

AREAS FOR IMPROVEMENT

Notes on my progress

GAME SCORES

Course:

Date: **Tee Off Time:**

Weather

Handicap: _____

Par: _____

Yardage: _____

Slope: _____

Rating: _____

Conditions: _____

Temperature: _____

Wind: _____

○ Casual

○ Competition

○ 9 Holes

○ 18 Holes

Players

_____

_____

_____

Front 9

	1	2	3	4	5	6	7	8	9	TOTAL	SUMS
PAR											
SCORE											
TEE BOX											
YARDS											
FW											
GIRs											
U&D											
PUTTS											
PENALTIES											

Back 9

	1	2	3	4	5	6	7	8	9	TOTAL	SUMS
PAR											
SCORE											
TEE BOX											
YARDS											
FW											
GIRs											
U&D											
PUTTS											
PENALTIES											

Notes about this Course

Notes about my Performance

Notes from the 19th Hole

GAME SCORES

Course:

Date: Tee Off Time:

Weather

Handicap: _____

Par: _____

Yardage: _____

Slope: _____

Rating: _____

Conditions: _____

Temperature: _____

Wind: _____

○ Casual

○ Competition

○ 9 Holes

○ 18 Holes

Players

_____

_____

_____

_____

Front 9

	1	2	3	4	5	6	7	8	9	TOTAL	SUMS
PAR											
SCORE											
TEE BOX											
YARDS											
FW											
GIRs											
U&D											
PUTTS											
PENALTIES											

Back 9

	1	2	3	4	5	6	7	8	9	TOTAL	SUMS
PAR											
SCORE											
TEE BOX											
YARDS											
FW											
GIRs											
U&D											
PUTTS											
PENALTIES											

Notes about this Course

Notes about my Performance

Notes from the 19th Hole

GAME SCORES

Course:

Date: Tee Off Time:

Handicap: _____

Par: _____

Yardage: _____

Slope: _____

Rating: _____

Weather

Conditions: _____

Temperature: _____

Wind: _____

○ Casual
○ Competition
○ 9 Holes
○ 18 Holes

Players

_____

_____

_____

Front 9

	1	2	3	4	5	6	7	8	9	TOTAL	SUMS
PAR											
SCORE											
TEE BOX											
YARDS											
FW											
GIRs											
U&D											
PUTTS											
PENALTIES											

Back 9

	1	2	3	4	5	6	7	8	9	TOTAL	SUMS
PAR											
SCORE											
TEE BOX											
YARDS											
FW											
GIRs											
U&D											
PUTTS											
PENALTIES											

Notes about this Course

Notes about my Performance

Notes from the 19th Hole

GAME SCORES

Course:

Date: **Tee Off Time:**

Weather

Handicap: _____

Par: _____

Yardage: _____

Slope: _____

Rating: _____

Conditions: _____

Temperature: _____

Wind: _____

○ Casual

○ Competition

○ 9 Holes

○ 18 Holes

Players

_____

_____

_____

_____

Front 9

	1	2	3	4	5	6	7	8	9	TOTAL	SUMS
PAR											
SCORE											
TEE BOX											
YARDS											
FW											
GIRs											
U&D											
PUTTS											
PENALT-IES											

Back 9

	1	2	3	4	5	6	7	8	9	TOTAL	SUMS
PAR											
SCORE											
TEE BOX											
YARDS											
FW											
GIRs											
U&D											
PUTTS											
PENALT-IES											

Notes about this Course

Notes about my Performance

Notes from the 19th Hole

GAME SCORES

Course:

Date: Tee Off Time:

Weather

Handicap: _____

Par: _____

Yardage: _____

Slope: _____

Rating: _____

Conditions: _____

Temperature: _____

Wind: _____

○ Casual

○ Competition

○ 9 Holes

○ 18 Holes

Players

_____

_____

_____

_____

Front 9

	1	2	3	4	5	6	7	8	9	TOTAL	SUMS
PAR											
SCORE											
TEE BOX											
YARDS											
FW											
GIRs											
U&D											
PUTTS											
PENALTIES											

Back 9

	1	2	3	4	5	6	7	8	9	TOTAL	SUMS
PAR											
SCORE											
TEE BOX											
YARDS											
FW											
GIRs											
U&D											
PUTTS											
PENALTIES											

Notes about this Course

Notes about my Performance

Notes from the 19th Hole

GAME SCORES

Course:

Date: Tee Off Time:

Weather

Handicap: _____

Par: _____

Yardage: _____

Slope: _____

Rating: _____

Conditions: _____

Temperature: _____

Wind: _____

○ Casual

○ Competition

○ 9 Holes

○ 18 Holes

Players

_____

_____

_____

_____

Front 9

	1	2	3	4	5	6	7	8	9	TOTAL	SUMS
PAR											
SCORE											
TEE BOX											
YARDS											
FW											
GIRs											
U&D											
PUTTS											
PENALTIES											

Back 9

	1	2	3	4	5	6	7	8	9	TOTAL	SUMS
PAR											
SCORE											
TEE BOX											
YARDS											
FW											
GIRs											
U&D											
PUTTS											
PENALTIES											

Notes about this Course

Notes about my Performance

Notes from the 19th Hole

GAME SCORES

Course:

Date: **Tee Off Time:**

Weather

Handicap: _____

Par: _____

Yardage: _____

Slope: _____

Rating: _____

Conditions: _____

Temperature: _____

Wind: _____

- ○ Casual
- ○ Competition
- ○ 9 Holes
- ○ 18 Holes

Players

_____

_____

_____

Front 9

	1	2	3	4	5	6	7	8	9	TOTAL	SUMS
PAR											
SCORE											
TEE BOX											
YARDS											
FW											
GIRs											
U&D											
PUTTS											
PENALTIES											

Back 9

	1	2	3	4	5	6	7	8	9	TOTAL	SUMS
PAR											
SCORE											
TEE BOX											
YARDS											
FW											
GIRs											
U&D											
PUTTS											
PENALTIES											

Notes about this Course

Notes about my Performance

Notes from the 19th Hole

GAME SCORES

Course:

Date: _____ Tee Off Time: _____

Weather

Handicap: _____
Par: _____
Yardage: _____
Slope: _____
Rating: _____

Conditions: _____
Temperature: _____
Wind: _____

○ Casual
○ Competition
○ 9 Holes
○ 18 Holes

Players

_____
_____
_____

Front 9

	1	2	3	4	5	6	7	8	9	TOTAL	SUMS
PAR											
SCORE											
TEE BOX											
YARDS											
FW											
GIRs											
U&D											
PUTTS											
PENALTIES											

Back 9

	1	2	3	4	5	6	7	8	9	TOTAL	SUMS
PAR											
SCORE											
TEE BOX											
YARDS											
FW											
GIRs											
U&D											
PUTTS											
PENALTIES											

Notes about this Course

_____
_____
_____
_____
_____
_____
_____
_____
_____

Notes about my Performance

_____
_____
_____
_____
_____
_____
_____
_____
_____
_____
_____

Notes from the 19th Hole

GAME SCORES

Course:

Date: **Tee Off Time:**

Weather

Conditions: _____

Temperature: _____

Wind: _____

Handicap: _____

Par: _____

Yardage: _____

Slope: _____

Rating: _____

○ Casual

○ Competition

○ 9 Holes

○ 18 Holes

Players

_____

_____

_____

_____

Front 9

	1	2	3	4	5	6	7	8	9	TOTAL	SUMS
PAR											
SCORE											
TEE BOX											
YARDS											
FW											
GIRs											
U&D											
PUTTS											
PENALTIES											

Back 9

	1	2	3	4	5	6	7	8	9	TOTAL	SUMS
PAR											
SCORE											
TEE BOX											
YARDS											
FW											
GIRs											
U&D											
PUTTS											
PENALTIES											

Notes about this Course

Notes about my Performance

Notes from the 19th Hole

GAME SCORES

Course:

Date: **Tee Off Time:**

Weather

Handicap: _____

Par: _____

Yardage: _____

Slope: _____

Rating: _____

Conditions: _____

Temperature: _____

Wind: _____

- ○ Casual
- ○ Competition
- ○ 9 Holes
- ○ 18 Holes

Players

_____
_____
_____
_____

Front 9

	1	2	3	4	5	6	7	8	9	TOTAL	SUMS
PAR											
SCORE											
TEE BOX											
YARDS											
FW											
GIRs											
U&D											
PUTTS											
PENALTIES											

Back 9

	1	2	3	4	5	6	7	8	9	TOTAL	SUMS
PAR											
SCORE											
TEE BOX											
YARDS											
FW											
GIRs											
U&D											
PUTTS											
PENALTIES											

Notes about this Course

Notes about my Performance

Notes from the 19th Hole

GAME SCORES

Course:

Date: _____ **Tee Off Time:** _____

Weather

Handicap: _____
Par: _____
Yardage: _____
Slope: _____
Rating: _____

Conditions: _____
Temperature: _____
Wind: _____

○ Casual
○ Competition
○ 9 Holes
○ 18 Holes

Players
_____
_____
_____

Front 9

	1	2	3	4	5	6	7	8	9	TOTAL	SUMS
PAR											
SCORE											
TEE BOX											
YARDS											
FW											
GIRs											
U&D											
PUTTS											
PENALTIES											

Back 9

	1	2	3	4	5	6	7	8	9	TOTAL	SUMS
PAR											
SCORE											
TEE BOX											
YARDS											
FW											
GIRs											
U&D											
PUTTS											
PENALTIES											

Notes about this Course

Notes about my Performance

Notes from the 19th Hole

GAME SCORES

Course:

Date: Tee Off Time:

Weather

Handicap: _____

Par: _____

Yardage: _____

Slope: _____

Rating: _____

Conditions: _____

Temperature: _____

Wind: _____

- ○ Casual
- ○ Competition
- ○ 9 Holes
- ○ 18 Holes

Players

_____

_____

_____

_____

Front 9

	1	2	3	4	5	6	7	8	9	TOTAL	SUMS
PAR											
SCORE											
TEE BOX											
YARDS											
FW											
GIRs											
U&D											
PUTTS											
PENALTIES											

Back 9

	1	2	3	4	5	6	7	8	9	TOTAL	SUMS
PAR											
SCORE											
TEE BOX											
YARDS											
FW											
GIRs											
U&D											
PUTTS											
PENALTIES											

Notes about this Course

Notes about my Performance

Notes from the 19th Hole

GAME SCORES

Course:

Date: Tee Off Time:

Weather

Handicap: _____

Par: _____

Yardage: _____

Slope: _____

Rating: _____

Conditions: _____

Temperature: _____

Wind: _____

- ○ Casual
- ○ Competition
- ○ 9 Holes
- ○ 18 Holes

Players

_____

_____

_____

_____

Front 9

	1	2	3	4	5	6	7	8	9	TOTAL	SUMS
PAR											
SCORE											
TEE BOX											
YARDS											
FW											
GIRs											
U&D											
PUTTS											
PENALTIES											

Back 9

	1	2	3	4	5	6	7	8	9	TOTAL	SUMS
PAR											
SCORE											
TEE BOX											
YARDS											
FW											
GIRs											
U&D											
PUTTS											
PENALTIES											

Notes about this Course

Notes about my Performance

Notes from the 19th Hole

GAME SCORES

Course:

Date: **Tee Off Time:**

Weather

Handicap: _____

Par: _____

Yardage: _____

Slope: _____

Rating: _____

Conditions: _____

Temperature: _____

Wind: _____

○ Casual

○ Competition

○ 9 Holes

○ 18 Holes

Players
_____
_____
_____

Front 9

	1	2	3	4	5	6	7	8	9	TOTAL	SUMS
PAR											
SCORE											
TEE BOX											
YARDS											
FW											
GIRs											
U&D											
PUTTS											
PENALTIES											

Back 9

	1	2	3	4	5	6	7	8	9	TOTAL	SUMS
PAR											
SCORE											
TEE BOX											
YARDS											
FW											
GIRs											
U&D											
PUTTS											
PENALTIES											

Notes about this Course

Notes about my Performance

Notes from the 19th Hole

GAME SCORES

Course:

Date: Tee Off Time:

Weather

Handicap: _____

Par: _____

Yardage: _____

Slope: _____

Rating: _____

Conditions: _____

Temperature: _____

Wind: _____

○ Casual

○ Competition

○ 9 Holes

○ 18 Holes

Players

_____

_____

_____

Front 9

	1	2	3	4	5	6	7	8	9	TOTAL	SUMS
PAR											
SCORE											
TEE BOX											
YARDS											
FW											
GIRs											
U&D											
PUTTS											
PENALTIES											

Back 9

	1	2	3	4	5	6	7	8	9	TOTAL	SUMS
PAR											
SCORE											
TEE BOX											
YARDS											
FW											
GIRs											
U&D											
PUTTS											
PENALTIES											

Notes about this Course

Notes about my Performance

Notes from the 19th Hole

GAME SCORES

Course:

Date: **Tee Off Time:**

Weather

Handicap: _____

Par: _____

Yardage: _____

Slope: _____

Rating: _____

Conditions: _____

Temperature: _____

Wind: _____

○ Casual

○ Competition

○ 9 Holes

○ 18 Holes

Players

_____

_____

_____

Front 9

	1	2	3	4	5	6	7	8	9	TOTAL	SUMS
PAR											
SCORE											
TEE BOX											
YARDS											
FW											
GIRs											
U&D											
PUTTS											
PENALTIES											

Back 9

	1	2	3	4	5	6	7	8	9	TOTAL	SUMS
PAR											
SCORE											
TEE BOX											
YARDS											
FW											
GIRs											
U&D											
PUTTS											
PENALTIES											

Notes about this Course

Notes about my Performance

Notes from the 19th Hole

GAME SCORES

Course:

Date: Tee Off Time:

Weather

Handicap: _____

Par: _____

Yardage: _____

Slope: _____

Rating: _____

Conditions: _____

Temperature: _____

Wind: _____

○ Casual

○ Competition

○ 9 Holes

○ 18 Holes

Players
_____
_____
_____
_____

Front 9

	1	2	3	4	5	6	7	8	9	TOTAL	SUMS
PAR											
SCORE											
TEE BOX											
YARDS											
FW											
GIRs											
U&D											
PUTTS											
PENALTIES											

Back 9

	1	2	3	4	5	6	7	8	9	TOTAL	SUMS
PAR											
SCORE											
TEE BOX											
YARDS											
FW											
GIRs											
U&D											
PUTTS											
PENALTIES											

Notes about this Course

Notes about my Performance

Notes from the 19th Hole

Tournaments

TOURNAMENT TRACKER

Date	Tournament	Course	Entry Fee	Entry Closing Date	Entered ✓

EVENT STATS

Event: _____

Course: _____

Date: _____ **Tee Off Time:** _____

Entry Fee: _____ **Prize:** _____

In Field ◯   Position Finished ◯

Yardage: _____
Slope: _____
Rating: _____

◯ Individual
◯ Four Ball
◯ 9 Holes
◯ 18 Holes

Weather Conditions: _____
Temperature: _____
Wind: _____

Players	Scores				
	Round	1	2	3	4
_____	Score				
_____	Finished				
_____	TOTAL SCORE				
_____					

EVENT STATS

Event: _____

Course: _____

Date: _____ Tee Off Time: _____

Entry Fee: _____ Prize: _____

In Field   Position Finished

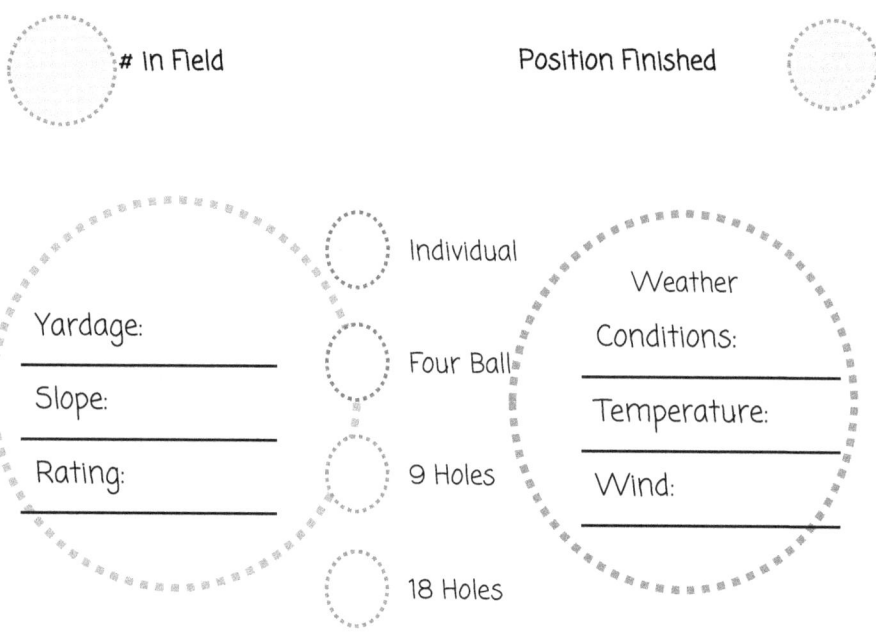

Yardage: _____

Slope: _____

Rating: _____

○ Individual

○ Four Ball

○ 9 Holes

○ 18 Holes

Weather Conditions: _____

Temperature: _____

Wind: _____

Players	Scores				
	Round	1	2	3	4
_____	Score				
_____	Finished				
_____	TOTAL SCORE				
_____					

Event: _____

Course: _____

Date: _____ **Tee Off Time:** _____

Entry Fee: _____ **Prize:** _____

In Field _____ Position Finished _____

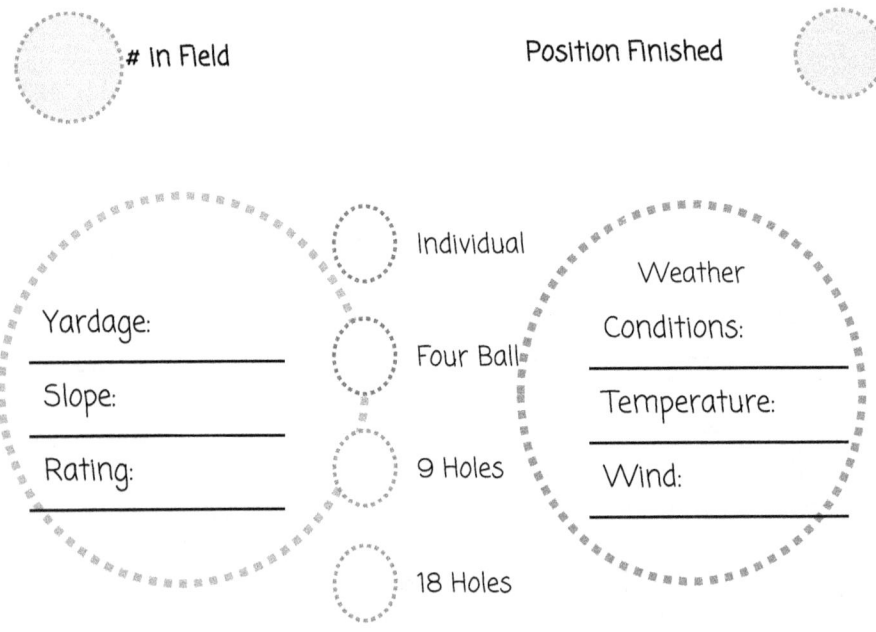

- Individual
- Four Ball
- 9 Holes
- 18 Holes

Yardage: _____
Slope: _____
Rating: _____

Weather Conditions: _____
Temperature: _____
Wind: _____

Players	Scores				
	Round	1	2	3	4
_____	Score				
_____	Finished				
_____	TOTAL SCORE				
_____					

EVENT STATS

Event: _____

Course: _____

Date: _____ Tee Off Time: _____

Entry Fee: _____ Prize: _____

In Field   Position Finished

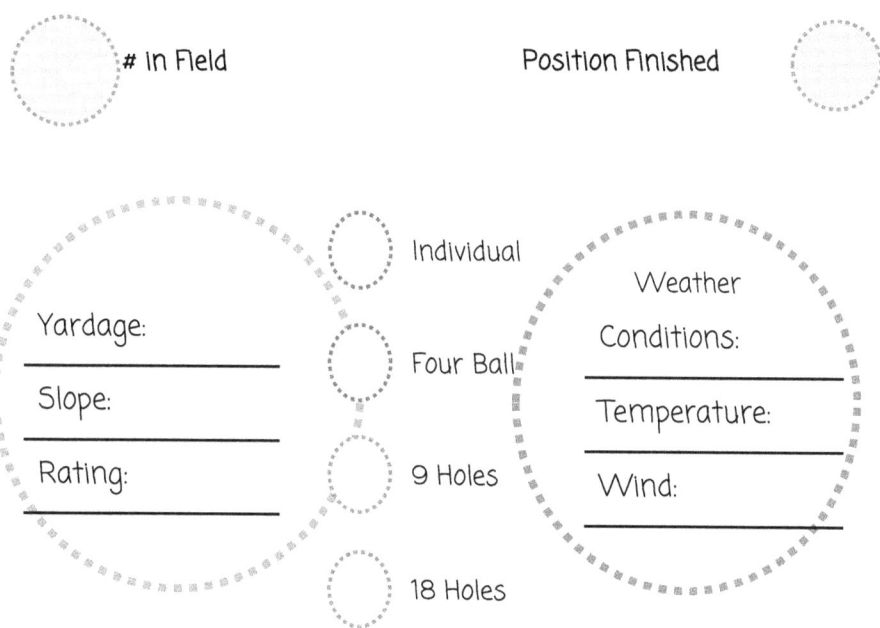

Yardage: _____

Slope: _____

Rating: _____

○ Individual

○ Four Ball

○ 9 Holes

○ 18 Holes

Weather Conditions: _____

Temperature: _____

Wind: _____

Players	Scores				
	Round	1	2	3	4
_____	Score				
_____	Finished				
_____	TOTAL SCORE				
_____					

EVENT STATS

Event: _____

Course: _____

Date: _____ Tee Off Time: _____

Entry Fee: _____ Prize: _____

In Field   Position Finished

Yardage: _____
Slope: _____
Rating: _____

○ Individual
○ Four Ball
○ 9 Holes
○ 18 Holes

Weather Conditions: _____
Temperature: _____
Wind: _____

Players	Scores				
	Round	1	2	3	4
_____	Score				
_____	Finished				
_____	TOTAL SCORE				
_____					

Event:

Course:

Date: Tee Off Time:

Entry Fee: Prize:

In Field   Position Finished

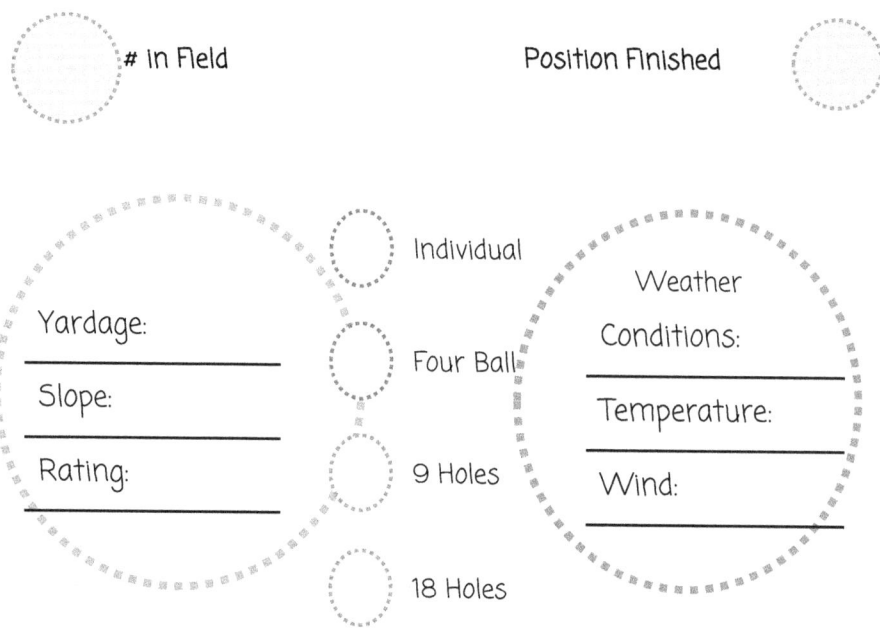

Yardage:

Slope:

Rating:

Individual

Four Ball

9 Holes

18 Holes

Weather Conditions:

Temperature:

Wind:

Players	Scores				
	Round	1	2	3	4
	Score				
	Finished				
	TOTAL SCORE				

EVENT STATS

Event: _____

Course: _____

Date: _____ Tee Off Time: _____

Entry Fee: _____ Prize: _____

In Field   Position Finished

Yardage: _____
Slope: _____
Rating: _____

○ Individual
○ Four Ball
○ 9 Holes
○ 18 Holes

Weather Conditions: _____
Temperature: _____
Wind: _____

Players	Scores				
	Round	1	2	3	4
_____	Score				
_____	Finished				
_____	TOTAL SCORE				
_____					

EVENT STATS

Event: _____

Course: _____

Date: _____ Tee Off Time: _____

Entry Fee: _____ Prize: _____

In Field _____   Position Finished _____

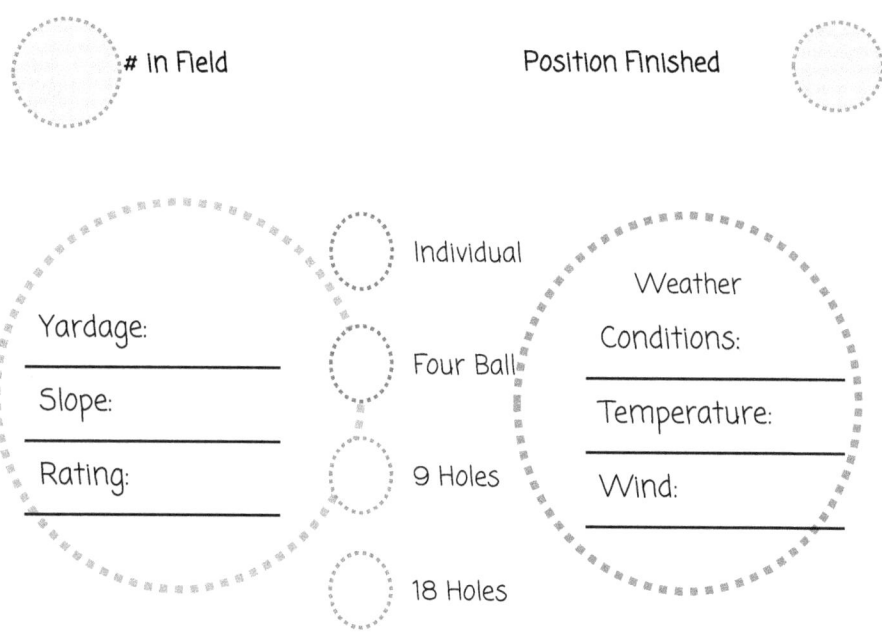

- Individual
- Four Ball
- 9 Holes
- 18 Holes

Yardage: _____

Slope: _____

Rating: _____

Weather Conditions: _____

Temperature: _____

Wind: _____

Players	Scores				
	Round	1	2	3	4
_____	Score				
_____	Finished				
_____	TOTAL SCORE				
_____					

EVENT STATS

Event: _____

Course: _____

Date: _____ Tee Off Time: _____

Entry Fee: _____ Prize: _____

In Field   Position Finished

Yardage: _____
Slope: _____
Rating: _____

○ Individual
○ Four Ball
○ 9 Holes
○ 18 Holes

Weather Conditions: _____
Temperature: _____
Wind: _____

Players	Scores				
	Round	1	2	3	4
_____	Score				
_____	Finished				
_____	TOTAL SCORE				

EVENT STATS

Event: _____

Course: _____

Date: _____ **Tee Off Time:** _____

Entry Fee: _____ **Prize:** _____

In Field   Position Finished

Yardage: _____
Slope: _____
Rating: _____

- Individual
- Four Ball
- 9 Holes
- 18 Holes

Weather Conditions: _____
Temperature: _____
Wind: _____

Players	Scores				
	Round	1	2	3	4
_____	Score				
_____	Finished				
_____	TOTAL SCORE				
_____					

Date	Details	Budget	Actual
	Clothing		
	Equipment		
	Tournaments		
	Sponsorships		
	19th Hole		

Expenses

Date	Details	Budget	Actual
	Clothing		
	Equipment		
	Tournaments		
	Sponsorships		
	19th Hole		

Expenses

Date	Details	Budget	Actual
	Clothing		
	Equipment		
	Tournaments		
	Sponsorships		
	19th Hole		

Expenses

Date	Details	Budget	Actual
	Clothing		
	Equipment		
	Tournaments		
	Sponsorships		
	19th Hole		

Expenses

Date	Details	Budget	Actual
	Clothing		
	Equipment		
	Tournaments		
	Sponsorships		
	19th Hole		

Expenses

Date	Details	Budget	Actual
	Clothing		
	Equipment		
	Tournaments		
	Sponsorships		
	19th Hole		

Expenses

Date	Details	Budget	Actual
	Clothing		
	Equipment		
	Tournaments		
	Sponsorships		
	19th Hole		

Expenses

Date	Details	Budget	Actual
	Clothing		
	Equipment		
	Tournaments		
	Sponsorships		
	19th Hole		

www.ingramcontent.com/pod-product-compliance
Lightning Source LLC
Chambersburg PA
CBHW070854050426
42453CB00012B/2196